My First Book of
SPACE

ARCTURUS

ARCTURUS

This edition published in 2019 by Arcturus Publishing Limited
26/27 Bickels Yard, 151–153 Bermondsey Street,
London SE1 3HA

Author: Claire Philip
Illustrator: Jean Claude
Designer: Sally Bond
Editors: Donna Gregory and Violet Peto

ISBN: 978-1-78888-489-1
CH006558NT
Supplier 29, Date 0619, Print run 8367

Printed in China

CONTENTS

STARRY NIGHT

Look up! There are so many stars in the sky. No one could count them all. It would take too long!

The stars look like tiny, twinkling dots of light.

If you connect the starry dots into groups, you can make pictures, such as a bear or a swan.

Look through a telescope, and stars will seem bigger and brighter.

A star is a very big, very hot ball of gas. The gas is burning fiercely, and that makes the star very bright.

The Sun is a star, but it looks different from other stars because it is closer to us.

Stars are very, very far away. It would take thousands of years to travel to the nearest one.

Some stars are billions of years old. That's an awful lot of birthdays!

THE STARS ABOVE US

Our nearest star, the Sun, is just one of many billions of stars that make up the Milky Way. The Milky Way is a group of stars, called a galaxy.

On a very clear night, we can see this beautiful blanket of stars spread across the sky.

Ancient Romans called it the "road of milk," and ancient Greeks named it the "milky circle."

For a long time, people thought that ALL the stars were in the Milky Way, but we now know there are many, many more galaxies filled with all kinds of different stars.

Constellations are star patterns in the sky. You can use star maps to find them.

Orion is one of the most famous constellations. It can be seen throughout the whole world.

Earth is here

Constellations are useful because they help us recognize and find certain stars, for example, the North Star, which explorers used to find their way.

WHAT IS THE UNIVERSE?

When we look up into space, we are looking out into the Universe. It's billions of years old!

The Universe is EVERYTHING, including all the stars and planets and things we can see. It also includes all the things we can't see.

The Universe is growing outward, getting bigger all the time.

The Big Bang is the name experts use to describe the moment the Universe first formed in a huge explosion.

Scientists are trying to understand where we are in the Universe— are we on the edge or in the middle?

THE SOLAR SYSTEM

The solar system is a moving system of planets, moons, and other space objects.

Asteroid belt

Earth

Earth, like Mercury, Venus, and Mars, is a rocky planet.

Venus

Mercury

SUN

The Sun is in the middle of the solar system.

The Sun pulls the solar system's planets toward it. This keeps the planets from zooming off into outer space.

Jupiter

The planets travel
around the Sun
on paths
called orbits.

Neptune

The orbits
are different
shapes and
distances
from the Sun,
depending on
the planet.

Uranus

Jupiter, Saturn,
Uranus, and Neptune
are mostly made up
of gases, which means
we can't land on
their surface.

Mars

Saturn

HOW BIG?

Here are all of the planets in our solar system. Some of them are unimaginably big.

← Jupiter

Jupiter is the biggest planet.

Saturn

You could fit 1,321 planets the size of Earth inside Saturn.

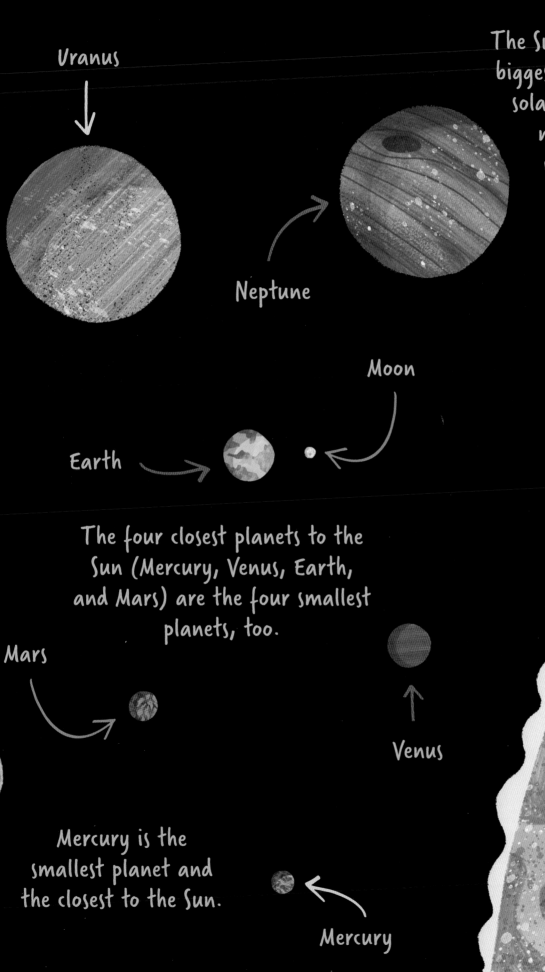

Uranus

The Sun is by far the biggest object in our solar system—it's nearly 10 times wider than the next biggest!

Neptune

Moon

Earth

SUN

The four closest planets to the Sun (Mercury, Venus, Earth, and Mars) are the four smallest planets, too.

Mars

Venus

Mercury is the smallest planet and the closest to the Sun.

Mercury

OUR LIFE-GIVING STAR

The Sun, our closest star, is an enormous ball of burning hot gas in space.

One of the main reasons we have life on Earth is the Sun—it gives us light and warmth.

The hot gas in the Sun is always moving. Solar flares are sudden bright flashes on the Sun's surface.

Scientists study the Sun to discover how it works and to understand more about other stars, too.

More than one million planet Earths would fit inside the Sun. It's enormous!

MERCURY: THE WRINKLY PLANET

The closest planet to the Sun, Mercury is the smallest planet in our solar system and is only a little bigger than Earth's Moon.

Mercury moves around the Sun very quickly. One year on the planet lasts the same amount of time as roughly 3 months on Earth.

It is named after the Roman god Mercury, a messenger who could travel at very fast speeds.

This planet looks as though it has wrinkles, but it is, in fact, covered with large ridges called scarps.

These scarps were formed as Mercury's core cooled, causing the planet to shrink.

Mercury is also covered in craters (huge dents caused by crashing space rocks).

One of the craters is named after a famous painter, Vincent Van Gogh.

Experts believe that ice may possibly exist inside the planet's craters.

17

VENUS: OUR SISTER PLANET

Venus, the second planet from the Sun, is also known as our sister planet.

This is because it is very similar in size to Earth and is also rocky.

Venus is much hotter than Earth, which means that humans could never live there.

It also has a thick, toxic atmosphere. This means that the layer of gases that covers the planet would be deadly for us to breathe.

It can be seen from Earth on a clear night, as its surface is lit up so brightly by the Sun.

Venus stands out in the night sky because its light is steady, not twinkly like the stars. Can you spot it?

One day on Venus is very long—the same as 243 Earth days!

Venus is named after the Roman goddess of love and beauty.

The Earth gives us air to breathe and a protective layer of gas that covers the planet like a blanket. The Sun gives us light and heat.

Nearly three-quarters of Earth's surface is covered in water.

From snow-capped mountains and sun-drenched deserts, to bright coral reefs and green rain forests—life on Earth is beautiful.

Our seas, rivers, and lakes are full of life. If our oceans are healthy, it helps keep our planet healthy.

EARTH: OUR PLACE IN SPACE

The largest rocky planet, and third planet from the Sun is our home—planet Earth.

Scientists build amazing machines that can leave Earth and travel into space.

Earth is often called a goldilocks planet because conditions here are "just right" for life to exist.

Satellites travel around and around the Earth. Rockets are vehicles that can carry people to satellites, the Moon, or distant planets!

MOON: LUNAR LIFE

The Moon is a huge ball of space rock.

The Moon is a satellite, a space object that follows a path around a planet—Earth!

Scientists think that the Moon may have formed billions of years ago.

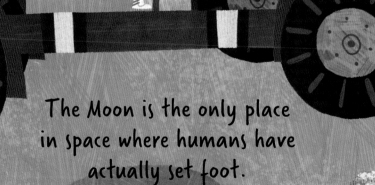

The Moon is the only place in space where humans have actually set foot.

As the Moon travels around Earth, the part of the Moon that faces the Sun is lit up.

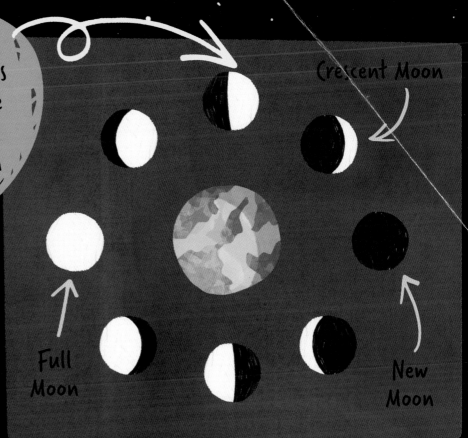

Crescent Moon

Full Moon

New Moon

The Moon appears to change shape throughout each month. These changes are called phases.

Each year, the Moon moves a little farther away from us.

Many of the markings, known as craters, on the Moon's surface, can be spotted from Earth.

Other planets have moons, too, but not all. Our Moon is the fifth-largest in our solar system.

MARS: THE RED PLANET

The fourth planet from the Sun, Mars is also known as the red planet. Its rocky surface is covered in an orange-red dust.

Named after the Roman god of war, this planet is about half the size of Earth.

Scientists believe that there may be salty water on its surface. Perhaps there was once life on Mars!

Like Earth, Mars is covered in ice at its north and south poles.

It would be very hard for people to live on this freezing-cold planet. However scientists are looking into whether it may be possible for humans to live there in the future.

The highest mountain in the solar system is here— Olympus Mons.

Sometimes we can see Mars glowing in the night sky from Earth.

It is almost three times as high as the highest mountain on Earth.

Special spacecraft called rovers have been to the surface of Mars to send information home. That's one of the ways we know so much about this planet.

Jupiter is named after the Roman king of the gods.

The swirls on Jupiter's outer surface look beautiful. However, they would be deadly to breathe.

There are many storms on Jupiter, such as the Great Red Spot. This hurricane is bigger than Earth and has been going for almost 200 years!

JUPITER: THE BIGGEST OF ALL

Jupiter, the fifth planet from the Sun, is the largest planet in our solar system.

It would be impossible to stand on the surface of this great gas giant, because it isn't solid.

Jupiter is more than twice the size of all of the other planets put together.

Jupiter has an incredible 67 moons in its orbit.

The largest of all, Ganymede, is even bigger than Mercury.

SATURN: THE JEWEL OF THE SOLAR SYSTEM

Saturn is the sixth planet from the Sun. It is famous for the many sparkling rings that circle around its middle.

These rings are made up of broken pieces of icy space rock. They were first spotted by famous astronomer Galileo hundreds of years ago.

Saturn is named after the god of farming in ancient Rome.

Of Saturn's 62 moons, Titan is the biggest. It is the second-biggest moon in the entire solar system.

Titan is the only other space object with clouds, like Earth. It has its own atmosphere like a planet.

Like Jupiter, the beautiful planet Saturn is a gas giant.

Saturn is made of gas, so it is very light. If it was placed in a GIANT bowl of water, it would float!

URANUS: THE ICE GIANT

While it very slowly travels around the Sun, Uranus looks like a ball rolling on its side.

Uranus is the seventh planet from the Sun and the third gas giant. Like Saturn, it, too has rings.

Uranus' rings run from its top to its bottom. This makes it look like it has tipped over.

It is made up of different gases to Jupiter and Saturn, and is much more icy.

It was the first planet discovered using a telescope, rather than the naked eye. It was almost named George, after the king of England at the time!

The 27 moons of Uranus are mostly named after characters in plays by the famous playwright, William Shakespeare.

Instead, and more sensibly, it was named after a Greek god of the sky.

One of the most famous moons, Miranda, is covered in icy canyons.

NEPTUNE: THE BLUE PLANET

At the edge of our solar system is Neptune, the eighth planet. It is also the final gas giant.

It is very windy on Neptune. These winds reach far higher speeds than those on Earth.

Through a telescope,
Neptune glows a
beautiful bright blue.
It is named after the
Roman god of the sea.

Neptune's biggest moon
is Triton. Unusually,
it spins in the opposite
direction to all of
Neptune's other moons.

Neptune has rings running
around its middle, perhaps made
from other smashed-up space
rocks that came too close.

DWARF PLANETS

A dwarf planet is similar to a true planet in many ways.

What makes dwarf planets different is mostly that they are smaller than main planets.

Like the main planets, dwarf planets travel around the Sun in an orbit.

Dysnomia
(Eris's moon)

Eris is the farthest dwarf planet from the Sun.

We used to think Pluto was a main planet, but scientists changed their minds and decided it was a dwarf planet instead.

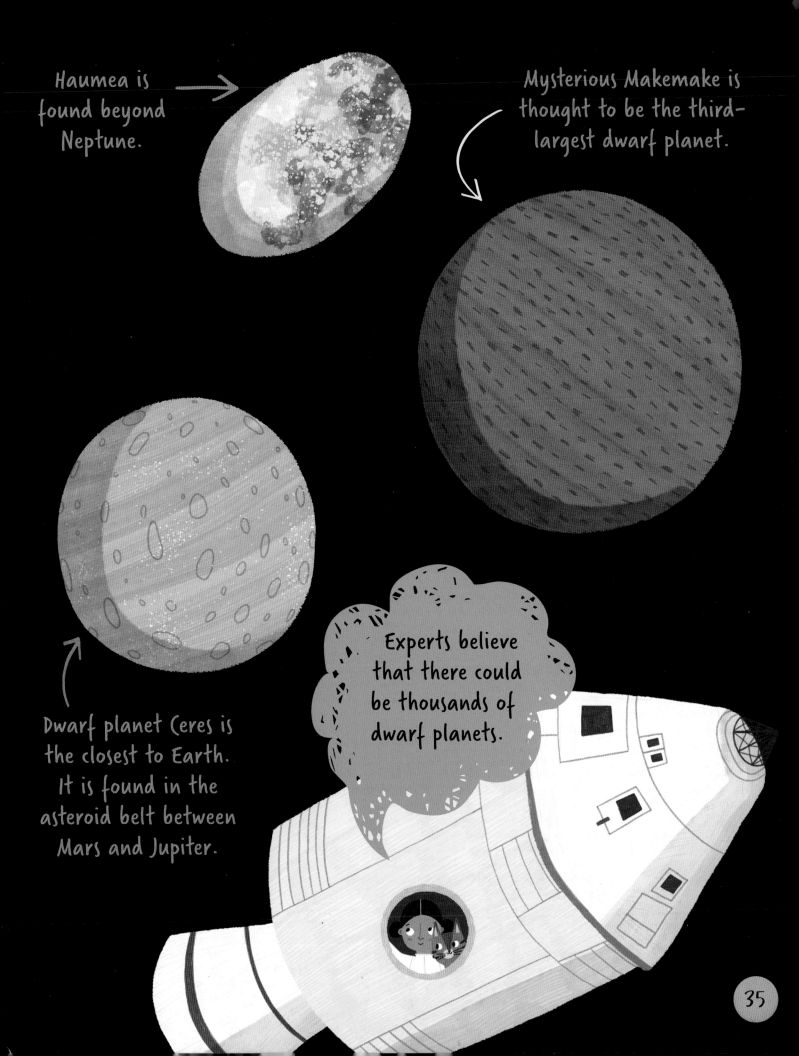

Haumea is found beyond Neptune.

Mysterious Makemake is thought to be the third-largest dwarf planet.

Dwarf planet Ceres is the closest to Earth. It is found in the asteroid belt between Mars and Jupiter.

Experts believe that there could be thousands of dwarf planets.

COMETS, ASTEROIDS, AND METEORS

As well as planets and moons, space is full of different kinds of space rock.

Comets are big pieces of rock and ice that whirl around the Sun.

Behind them, comets trail a tail made of gas. It can be hundreds —or even thousands—of miles long.

Asteroids are pieces of space rock that can be just a few feet in length—or big enough to have their own moons.

Between Mars and Jupiter is a huge band of thousands of asteroids.

Vesta is one of the largest asteroids. It is like a small, rocky planet.

This picture shows how different types of space rock look when viewed from space.

Comet

Earth

Asteroid

Meteors

Meteors are smaller pieces of rock. If they come close to the Earth, they burn up as they fall to the ground. Then, they are known as shooting stars.

SPACE TELESCOPES

Telescopes let us see farther into space than we can see with just our eyes. Some are based on Earth, but some have been sent into space.

Telescopes in space can see farther than telescopes on Earth.

The Hubble Space Telescope showed that in just one small area of space, there were more than 5,500 galaxies.

Galileo invented the first simple telescope more than 400 years ago!

Across Earth today, there are many huge telescopes, such as Keck 1 and Keck 2 on the Island of Hawaii.

These enormous telescopes make distant stars easy to see and study.

The James Webb Space Telescope is a new telescope set to be sent into space. It will be able to take photos farther into space than ever before.

SPACE TRAVEL

To send a spacecraft into space, scientists use a launch vehicle, or rocket.

Rockets have incredibly powerful engines. These help them reach speeds fast enough to leave Earth's atmosphere.

They burn lots of fuel, which gives them enough energy to move.

The Space Shuttle is one of the most famous spacecrafts ever. Now retired, it flew 135 missions and carried seven astronauts each time.

It is easiest to launch craft into space from near the equator, the invisible line around Earth.

The new and improved Space Launch System (SLS) will soon be in use. It may take astronauts to Mars for the first time ever.

The Space Shuttle

One spacecraft, Kepler, has been sent out of our solar system to find new planet systems. More and more are discovered all the time!

THE INTERNATIONAL SPACE STATION

Many nations from across the world came together to build this amazing space station.

The International Space Station (ISS) orbits Earth.

Astronauts eat three meals a day. They eat with knives and forks, like we do on Earth. But they don't eat outside the station of course!

The ISS was built so that astronauts could do scientific experiments in space. They look at what happens to our bodies when we are in space, for example.

The ISS is as long as a football stadium. You can sometimes see it zooming across the sky! It looks like a very fast-moving plane.

On the ISS, astronauts have to exercise for two hours each day to stay fit. Otherwise, their muscles and bones would get weak very quickly.

43

QUIZ: TRUE OR FALSE?

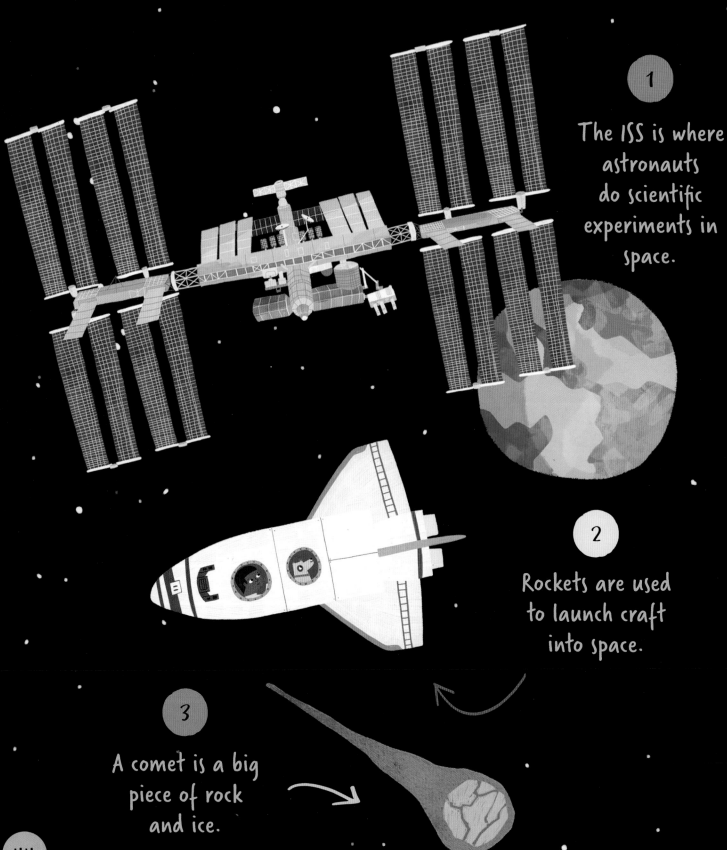

1
The ISS is where astronauts do scientific experiments in space.

2
Rockets are used to launch craft into space.

3
A comet is a big piece of rock and ice.

4

Asteroids can be
large enough to have
their own moons.

5

Haumea is the closest
planet to the Sun.

6

Neptune is a bright
pink planet.

Answers on page 47

QUIZ CONTINUED

7 Uranus is a rocky planet.

8 The Great Red Spot is a storm on Jupiter.

9 Olympus Mons is the highest mountain in the solar system.

10

The planet Venus can be seen from Earth.

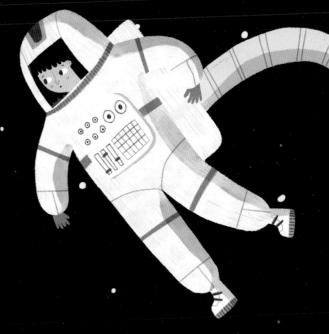

11

Mercury is the farthest planet from the Sun.

12

The Moon is the only place in space where humans have actually set foot.

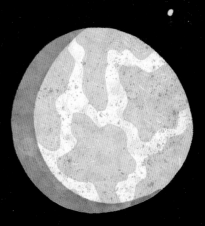

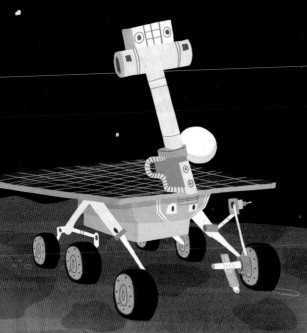

ANSWERS:

Answers: 1. True. 2. True. 3. True. 4. True. 5. False—it is a dwarf planet that is found beyond Neptune. 6. False—it appears blue. 7. False— it is gassy. 8. True. 9. True. 10. True. 11. False— it is the closet planet to the Sun. 12. True.

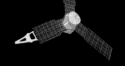

GLOSSARY

ASTEROID   A small, rocky space object.

ATMOSPHERE   A shell of gases around a planet, star, or other object.

COMET   A chunk of rock and ice from the edge of the solar system. When it is close to the Sun, its melting ices form a tail.

CONSTELLATION   A star pattern in the sky.

CRATER   A big hole in the ground.

GALAXY   A huge collection of stars, gases, and dust.

HURRICANE   A very large, swirling, and windy storm.

MILKY WAY   Our home galaxy.

MOON   A ball of rock that travels around Earth.

ORBIT   The path that an object in space takes around another space object.

PLANET   A huge, round object that travels around a star.

ROVER   A space robot that can move across the surface of a planet. It sends pictures and information about other planets to scientists.

SATELLITE   Any object that travels around a planet. Moons are satellites made of rock and ice. Satellites can also be machines in orbit around Earth.

STAR   A giant ball of hot gas. Most stars look small in the sky because they are so far away.

SUN   Our closest star, in the middle of the solar system.

UNIVERSE   Everything around us, including the world, space, and everything in it.